WOMEN IN THE WORLD OF SOUTHEAST ASIA

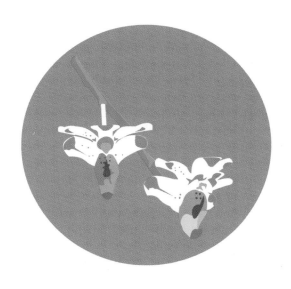

WOMEN'S ISSUES:
GLOBAL TRENDS

Women in the Arab World

Women in the World of Japan

Women in the World of Africa

Women in the World of China

Native Women in the Americas

Women in the World of India

Women in the Eastern European World

Women in the World of Southeast Asia

Women in the Hispanic World

Women in the World of Russia

Women in the Mediterranean World

Women in North America's Religious World

WOMEN'S ISSUES: GLOBAL TRENDS

WOMEN IN THE WORLD OF SOUTHEAST ASIA

BY
AUTUMN LIBAL

Mason Crest Publishers
Philadelphia

The author would like to thank Alexandra Ho for her valuable contribution to this book.

Mason Crest Publishers Inc.
370 Reed Road
Broomall, Pennsylvania 19008
(866) MCP-BOOK (toll free)

First printing.
1 2 3 4 5 6 7 8 9 10
ISBN 1-59084-867-5
ISBN 1-59084-856-X (series)

Library of Congress Cataloging-in-Publication Data

Libal, Autumn.
  Women in the world of Southeast Asia / by Autumn Libal.
     p. cm. — (Women's issues, global trends)
  Includes bibliographical references and index.
  ISBN 1-59084-867-5
  1. Women—Asia, Southeastern—Juvenile literature. 2. Sex role—Asia, Southeastern—Juvenile literature. I. Title. II. Series.
  HQ1745.8.L53 2005
  305.42'0959—dc22
                              2004003856

Interior design by Michelle Bouch and MK Bassett-Harvey.
Illustrations by Michelle Bouch.
Produced by Harding House Publishing Service, Inc.
Cover design by Benjamin Stewart.
Printed in India.

CONTENTS

INTRODUCTION

by Mary Jo Dudley

The last thirty years have been a time of great progress for women around the world. In some countries, especially where women have more access to education and work opportunities, the relationships between women and men have changed radically. The boundaries between men's roles and women's roles have been crossed, and women are enjoying many experiences that were denied them in past centuries.

But there is still much to be done. On the global stage, women are increasingly the ones who suffer most from poverty. At the same time that they produce 75 to 90 percent of the world's food crops, they are also responsible for taking care of their households. According to the United Nations, in no country in the world do men come anywhere near to spending as much time on housework as women do. This means that women's job opportunities are often extremely limited, contributing to the "feminization of poverty."

In fact, two out of every three poor adults are women. According to the Decade of Women, "Women do two-thirds of the world's work, receive 10 percent of the world's income, and own one percent of the means of production." Women often have no choice but to take jobs that lack long-term security or

adequate pay; many women work in dangerous working conditions or in unprotected home-based industries. This series clearly illustrates how historic events and contemporary trends (such as war, conflicts, and migration) have also contributed to women's loss of property and diminished access to resources.

A recent report from Human Rights Watch indicates that many countries continue to deny women basic legal protections. Amnesty International points out, "Governments are not living up to their promises under the Women's Convention to protect women from discrimination and violence such as rape and female genital mutilation." Many nations—including the United States—have not ratified the United Nations' Women's Treaty.

During times of armed conflict, especially under policies of ethnic cleansing, women are particularly at risk. Murder, torture, systematic rape, forced pregnancy and forced abortions are all too common human rights violations endured by women around the world. This series presents the experience of women in Vietnam, Cambodia, the Middle East, and other war torn regions.

In the political arena, equality between men and women has still not been achieved. Around the world, women are underrepresented in their local and national governments; on average, women represent only 10 percent of all legislators worldwide. This series provides excellent examples of key female leaders who have promoted women's rights and occupied unique leadership positions, despite historical contexts that would normally have shut them out from political and social prominence.

The Fourth World Conference on Women called upon the international community to take action in the following areas of concern:

- the persistent and increasing burden of poverty on women
- inequalities and inadequacies in access to education and training
- inequalities and inadequacies in access to health care and related services
- violence against women

- the effects of armed or other kinds of conflict on women
- inequality in economic structures and policies, in all forms of productive processes, and in access to resources
- insufficient mechanisms at all levels to promote the advancement of women
- lack of protection of women's human rights
- stereotyping of women and inequality in women's participation in all community systems, especially the media
- gender inequalities in the management of natural resources and the safeguarding of the environment
- persistent discrimination against and violation of the rights of female children

The Conference's mission statement includes these sentences: "Equality between women and men is a matter of human rights and a condition for social justice and is also a necessary and fundamental prerequisite for equality, development and peace. . . equality between women and men is a condition . . . for society to meet the challenges of the twenty-first century." This series provides examples of how women have risen above adversity, despite their disadvantaged social, economic, and political positions.

Each book in WOMEN'S ISSUES: GLOBAL TRENDS takes a look at women's lives in a different key region or culture, revealing the history, contributions, triumphs, and challenges of women around the world. Women play key roles in shaping families, spirituality, and societies. By interweaving historic backdrops with the modern-day evolving role of women in the home and in society at large, this series presents the important part women play as cultural communicators. Protection of women's rights is an integral part of universal human rights, peace, and economic security. As a result, readers who gain understanding of women's lives around the world will have deeper insight into the current condition of global interactions.

"WOMEN, WITH THEIR CAPACITY FOR COMPASSION AND SELF-SACRIFICE, THEIR COURAGE AND PERSEVERANCE, HAVE DONE MUCH TO DISSIPATE THE DARKNESS OF INTOLERANCE AND HATE, SUFFERING AND DESPAIR."
—AUNG SAN SUU KYI

AN INTRODUCTION TO THE REGION

Between the waters of the Indian and Pacific oceans lies a tropical region of the world known as Southeast Asia. Southeast Asia is bordered on the west by India. To its north lies China. The region's neighbor to the south is Australia. Part of Southeast Asia is mainland, meaning it is connected to the larger Asian continent. The rest of Southeast Asia is made up of more than twenty thousand islands in the tropical waters of the South China Sea.

Like all areas and civilizations of the world, women have played and continue to play an important role in the development of Southeast Asia. The changes that have occurred in women's lives and roles in Southeast Asia have occurred against the backdrop of a very complicated history. Many of the struggles Southeast Asian women have faced cannot be understood without understanding the different historical changes that have affected their lives. A brief look at some of Southeast Asia's history will help explain this region, its people, and the experiences of women living in Southeast Asia today.

For many years, scholars believed that the first agricultural civilizations began in Mesopotamia (an ancient region in present-day Iraq) around 8000

B.C.E. and then spread to other regions. Arguments about the origins of civilization are *controversial*, and it is unclear whether agricultural civilizations in Southeast Asia began with the *aboriginal* people who already lived there or were introduced by migrating populations who came from places like India and China—areas that may have had earlier contact with agricultural civilizations like that in Mesopotamia. What we do know, however, is that throughout history, Southeast Asia's fertile, tropical land has been desirable to many people. Over time, millions of people from hundreds of different cultures would pass through or settle in these fertile lands. Some people came to Southeast Asia seeking wealth from the region's rich natural resources. Some came fleeing persecution in their native land. Some came to spread their religious beliefs. All

Southeast Asia is full of fertile lands and waterways.

WOMEN IN THE WORLD OF SOUTHEAST ASIA

Most people living in Southeast Asia today are descendants of people who originally came from areas like southern China and India rather than descendants of aboriginal groups. The Malay, Thai, and Khmer (all large populations in Southeast Asia today) are just a few examples of the many groups whose ancestors came from outside of Southeast Asia.

these people, their beliefs, and their ways of life have played a role in developing Southeast Asian society.

By 6000 B.C.E. agricultural practices had been adopted in coastal regions of the Southeast Asian mainland, and agricultural activities, once begun, led to the formation of certain ways of life. Unlike hunter-gatherer societies, many of which moved from place to place in search of the animals and plants they used for food, agricultural societies needed to stay in one place while crops grew. In these tribes and villages, the family was very important and was the basis for the social structure of the community.

As agriculture progressed, the most important crop came to be rice. Rice is now the *staple* food for much of the world, and there is some *archeological* evidence to suggest that Southeast Asia was actually the first place where rice was cultivated. Much of the rice in Southeast Asia is a variety that needs to be grown in flooded paddies. These *paddies* require irrigation systems, systems which can bring water to the paddies, sometimes over great distances. Irrigating the amazing networks of rice paddies required huge amounts of cooperation among families and communities. In some cases, growing rice also required that the land be dramatically altered to hold water. Many times, people in Southeast Asia had to cut *terraces* in hillsides to create the rice paddies. These terraces and irrigation systems were remarkable feats of engineering and technology in a time when technologies in many other parts of the world were not very advanced. Rice cultivation, and the technology and cooperation it required, strengthened Southeast Asian civilizations.

In addition to rice, Southeast Asian people grew numerous types of fruits, vegetables, and spices. Southeast Asia was also home to some of the first metalworking cultures. Metalworking began in the Southeast Asian mainland at least as early as 4000 B.C.E., and by 1000 B.C.E., trading of agricultural and technological goods was well-established throughout the region.

While Southeast Asia was growing in population and further developing as an agricultural and technological producer, its neighbors, India and China, were becoming the first great trading nations of the world. Southeast Asians had long been trading amongst themselves, using the region's many rivers as trading routes, but around A.D. 100, people from India and China also took interest in the agricultural products and other goods Southeast Asia produced. By approximately A.D. 700, Southeast Asia's first great *empires* were rising. The lands were filled with valuable resources, and many people sought to conquer and control these important centers of trade. As the centuries passed, empires grew, shrank, were conquered, grew again, and Southeast Asia was carved up in numerous different ways. If you travel around Southeast Asia today, you can see the ruins of incredible cities, monuments, and temples that were built by these empires of the past.

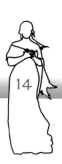

WOMEN IN THE WORLD OF SOUTHEAST ASIA

Life in the rural villages of Southeast Asia has changed very little down through the centuries.

As with so many other places around the world, European contact would have a major, permanent, and often-devastating impact on the people of Southeast Asia. In the late 1400s, European powers set out on a massive campaign to find and seize control of new lands and trading routes. They were specifically interested in the valuable and exotic spices that they knew came from the east. However, Europeans had very little knowledge about the world outside of Europe, and they weren't sure exactly where these spices came from. Thus, a race began between the European powers to discover the locations of and the fastest routes to these spices and other exotic goods.

The Portuguese were the first Europeans to gain control of Southeast Asian lands and trading routes. They conquered numerous islands and brought a new religion to these lands. At this time, Buddhism, Hinduism, and Islam (all religions that were brought into Southeast Asia by migrating populations or conquering armies) were already well established in many parts of the region. Now, however, the Portuguese brought Christianity.

The Spanish were the next Europeans to gain footholds in the region, taking many of the Portuguese lands and claiming what today is the Philippines. Soon after came the Dutch. The Dutch quickly became the most powerful of the European conquerors. They began the Dutch East India Company in 1602 and by the mid-1600s had succeeded in largely pushing the rest of the Portuguese out of the valuable Southeast Asian lands.

The British were the next to carve out Southeast Asian lands for their own. While the Dutch had control of the islands that would later become Indonesia, in the mid-1800s the British extended their reach from India into the portion of the Southeast Asian mainland that would become Burma. In this century, France also seized control of large portions of mainland Southeast Asia.

In 1898, the United States joined the colonial powers when it took the Philippines from the Spanish. The United States claimed to be fighting for the freedom of the colonized people and promised independence to the

Philippines. Upon winning the war, however, the United States did not relinquish control as promised and became much like the European powers in the region. With the Spanish removed, the remaining foreign powers in Southeast Asia were the British, French, Dutch, and the Americans.

For some people in areas that weren't readily *accessible* or desirable to the colonizers (such as mountain villages or areas that didn't have valuable farmland), life continued largely as it had before. Life for many Southeast-Asian people, however, changed greatly under colonial rule. For example, the colonizers ravaged Southeast Asia's forests for lumber and built huge plantations of crops like tea, coffee, rubber (which comes from trees), and tobacco to feed the *insatiable* European market. Many people lost their family land to these giant European farms and were forced to work for the Europeans instead of farming for themselves. To make matters worse, in the past both small Southeast-Asian communities and great trading empires always made sure there was enough rice to feed the local people before exporting rice for trade. The Europeans, however, didn't care if there was rice to feed the local populations. They only cared about exporting and selling as much rice as possible, so even in times when rice crops had high yields, Southeast-Asian communities still found themselves poor and starving.

The only Southeast Asian land not to be seized by European colonial powers was the area that today is Thailand, meaning "land of the free."

Rice in Southeast Asia is often grown on terraces like these.

The Europeans also brought huge numbers of laborers from India and China to work in the plantation fields. These laborers sent almost all their earnings home to the families they left behind. This led to conflicts between the newly arrived workers and the local populations. The local people could see that a great amount of money was being made from their land, but all that money was being funneled to Europe, India, and China instead of being reinvested in the local communities and economy. Sources of wealth that used to be controlled by the Southeast Asians were now completely controlled by other countries. In many cases, Southeast Asians could do little but watch themselves growing poorer while the Europeans grew wealthier. Europeans' plundering of Southeast-Asian lands, resources, and people continues to have a lasting effect on Southeast-Asian countries today.

World War I and World War II marked major turning points in the relationship between Southeast Asia and the colonial powers. During World War I, Germany, Austria-Hungary, Turkey, and Bulgaria invaded other European countries. In World War II, Germany, Japan, and Italy set forth on a similar quest for world domination. Fighting in the World Wars was not limited to Europe but spread all over the world to every place where European powers had colonies—including Southeast Asia.

World War I lasted from 1914 to 1918. During this time, the European powers turned to their colonies for support and troops. They said that this war was about freedom from *oppression* and the right to *self-governance*. Southeast Asian and other countries under colonial rule saw a *double standard* in what the British, French, Dutch, and Americans had to say. How was their colonizing and plundering of Southeast Asian lands different from Germany's aggression? Many Southeast Asians believed that if they supported the colonial powers during the war, then the colonial powers would have to address this double standard at war's end and give the Southeast Asian lands their independence.

The colonial powers realized the double standard as well and indeed promised to eventually give Southeast-Asian lands their independence, but these promises never materialized.

By the time World War II erupted in 1939, Southeast Asians were once again deeply *disillusioned* with the colonial powers. It was this disillusionment that led them to open their doors to another occupying power—Japan. In 1941, with the help of the Southeast Asians, Japanese forces swept across the whole of Southeast Asia driving the colonial powers out. But Japan had no intention of giving the Southeast Asian people their independence either, and by the time Japan was defeated in the war, the Southeast Asian colonies were ready to return to the bargaining table with the colonial powers. In the coming years, all of the Southeast-Asian nations would achieve independence. This did not mean peace for the Southeast-Asian people, however, for now a whole new round of struggles was about to begin.

Since gaining their independence, Southeast Asian countries have been plagued by conflict. Disagreements over what types of governments these countries should have and who should lead these governments have led to civil wars and some of the worst human-rights *atrocities* the world has ever seen. The fight against Communism tore Vietnam and Laos apart, and a communist regime in Cambodia ordered the killing of every educated person in the country and the emptying of the country's cities. A military dictatorship seized control in Myanmar, and Indonesia struggled as multiple areas demanded their own independence. Since the ending of World War II, millions of people in Southeast Asia have been killed or displaced in local wars and regional conflict. Despite much progress in the countries of Southeast Asia, many conflicts and disagreements continue today.

Today Southeast Asia is divided into eleven independent countries and is home to numerous *diverse* peoples. The mainland Southeast-Asian countries

A woman in Burma carries produce from the market.

If you live in the United States, you may hear people using the name Burma instead of Myanmar. This is because the United States government refuses to acknowledge the military dictatorship that seized Burma and changed its name to Myanmar as a legitimate government.

are Myanmar (Burma), Thailand, Lao People's Democratic Republic, Cambodia, Vietnam, and Singapore. The island countries are Indonesia, Brunei-Darussalam, the Philippines, and Timor-Leste (East Timor). The country of Malaysia is split. The western half of Malaysia is located on the mainland while the eastern half of Malaysia is part of the islands.

The United Nations estimates the 2005 population for Southeast Asia to be approximately 558,155,000 people. About 58.8 percent of the population lives in *rural* areas where life continues to be agriculturally based. For these people, many aspects of family and social life are much the same as they were hundreds of years ago. The other 41.2 percent of the population lives in *urban* areas. Life in the cities can be drastically different from life in the country. Women make up just over 50 percent of Southeast Asia's population.

Living conditions and economic prosperity in Southeast Asia today vary from area to area and country to country. In some places, people live in extreme poverty while in other places people have good-paying jobs. Some countries are

still struggling with the aftermath of war while other countries have promising economies.

Many of the major industries in Southeast Asia today continue to be based on the region's natural resources. Many people make their living through farming and fishing. Rubber, palm oil, tea, cocoa, and other cash crops continue to be important to the economy. Mining is also important with tin being one of the major mining industries. Southeast Asian lumber is exported throughout the world, and *Western* countries have become very interested in the oil-

A temple in Southeast Asia.

A woman in Myanmar (once called Burma) paddles a dugout boat.

production possibilities of some Southeast Asian countries. The agricultural, mining, lumber industries, and oil industries though playing a vital role in Southeast Asian economies have also caused significant environmental damage. Pollution, deforestation, erosion, and the poaching of endangered species are all major environmental problems for Southeast Asian nations.

Now that we understand a bit more about Southeast Asia, its history, and its people, we can begin to explore what women's lives are like in this region. In chapter 2, we will look at women's roles through history and see how they have changed in response to some of the situations we discussed here. In chapter 3, we will learn about women's lives in Southeast Asia today.

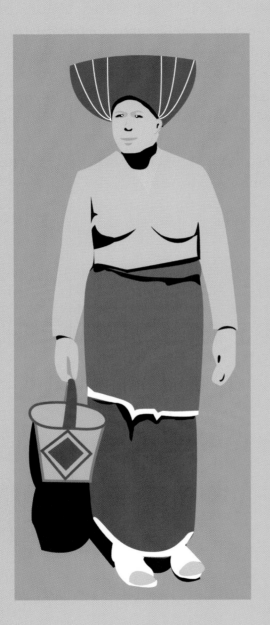

"[WOMEN'S ROLE] IN SHAPING THE VERY FABRIC OF OUR SOCIETY IS INTEGRAL TO THE HISTORY OF OUR NATION."
—H.E. MR SUDJADNAN PARNOHADININGRAT, AMBASSADOR OF THE REPUBLIC OF INDONESIA

THE HISTORICAL ROLES OF WOMEN IN SOUTHEAST ASIA

Since early times, Southeast Asian community structure has been matrilocal, meaning that the social structure was formed around the female side of the family. When a couple married, they went to live with the wife's family. A typical household consisted of the elderly parents, their daughters, the daughters' husbands, and the daughters' children. The sons would live in the households of their own wives. This matrilocal community structure continues in many rural areas of Southeast Asia today and forms a supportive community for women and children.

In Southeast Asian agricultural societies, women performed many of the same duties as men, most notably, working in the rice fields. Other tasks were often divided along gender lines, meaning men and women performed different types of work. As in other places in the world, women's work in early Southeast Asian civilizations focused not only on growing and harvesting food, but also on preparing food, making clothing and pottery, maintaining the household, raising the children, and caring for the elderly and sick. Activities like hunting, protection, warfare, and family and community leadership were

Women wash their families' clothes in the river.

mostly men's work. The oldest male in a household would have authority over the family, and a man would be chosen as the community's leader. Women, however, were not powerless. In many communities, it was the women's job to choose the community leader.

In Southeast Asia, women's role in managing the household also included managing the family's finances. When Southeast Asia grew to be trade-oriented, it was women who were in charge of trade. This may have occurred because women, as the managers of the household and household finances, were in the best position to know what goods (like food and cloth) the family had and whether there was a surplus of those goods that could be traded. The women would also know what goods the family needed and how much money would be required to purchase these goods. As time passed, women's role as financial managers became more and more entrenched in Southeast Asian society and would allow some Southeast Asian women to achieve levels of status and leadership rarely reached by women in other societies. Today, women in Southeast Asia continue to dominate trade and handle families' finances.

Unlike many other societies at the time in which only sons could inherit land, in Southeast Asian societies, land was inherited equally by both the sons and the daughters. Often, the youngest daughter would inherit the family home for it was the youngest daughter's duty to care for her parents in their old age. The ability to inherit property allowed women in Southeast-Asian society to have much more equality and independence than women in other parts of the world. Combined with Southeast Asian society's matrilocal structure, the ability to own land gave women a good deal of security. If a woman's husband died, fell ill, or left the family, for example, the woman and her children would not be abandoned with nothing. Instead, they would have the land that the woman owned and the support of the woman's family who they still lived with.

Striking examples of women's strength and independence can be seen in the leadership of a number of historic Southeast Asian states. As agriculture and

In Southeast-Asian society, it would not be unusual for a man to give all of his earnings to his wife. The woman would then decide what was needed for the family and would in turn give an allowance back to her husband for his own use. Some families continue to deal with finances in this way today.

world trade brought prosperity to Southeast Asian lands, a number of great states rose and fell. Despite the fact that men were traditionally at the head of the family and community, over time queens ruled many of these states.

One prosperous Southeast Asian state to adopt female rule was the port-state of Patani. In Patani, queens ruled for at least one hundred years beginning in 1584 when Raja Ijau, known as "the great queen," rose to power. Prior to Raja Ijau's rule, Patani had been politically unstable. During Ijau's thirty-two-year reign, however, Patani gained in organization, stability, and trade. After her death, Raja Ijau was followed by three more famous queens: "the blue queen" Raja Biru, "the purple queen" Raja Ungu, and "the yellow queen" Raja Kuning. We do not know much about the government of Patani after Raja Kuning's rule, but it is believed that queens continued to be appointed until at least the 1690s.

Another famous example of a prosperous state that was ruled, for a time, by women is Aceh. Between the sixteenth and seventeenth centuries, Aceh,

A woman in Thailand carries her child.

located on the northwestern tip of the island of Sumatra, was one of the most powerful trading centers in Southeast Asia. Between 1604 and 1637, a much loved but exceptionally brutal sultan, Iskandar Muda, ruled Aceh; Iskandar Muta killed anyone who threatened his rule. He even killed his own son. This created a problem for Aceh when Iskandar Muda died, for the only direct heir he left behind was his daughter. Iskandar Muda's son-in-law became the new leader, but when he too died in 1641, only Muda's daughter remained to take the throne. Thus, in 1641, Sultana Safiyyat ad-Din Taj al-Alam Syah, became Aceh's first female ruler.

Patani and Aceh provide striking historic examples of strong states under female rule, but they are certainly not the only examples of female rule in Southeast Asia. It is thought that, even though traditionally men were the heads of households and communities, women's role as financial managers made them good candidates for running a state. Because it was the women who managed finances, men were sometimes seen as irresponsible with money—clearly not a desirable quality in a future ruler. A common stereotype in Southeast Asia is that men are good at displaying wealth, but women are good at managing wealth.

WOMEN IN THE WORLD OF SOUTHEAST ASIA

Under Sultana Safiyyat ad-Din, Aceh became even more prosperous than it had been under her father. The sultana proved to be such a good ruler that, after her death, another woman was chosen to rule. Between 1641 and 1688, Aceh had four successive female rulers.

The fact that some women became leaders does not mean, however that women always held positions of strength, security, or even respect in Southeast Asian society. Women have had many struggles in Southeast Asia as well. As trade increased in Southeast Asia, many aspects of society changed. Certain groups of people became much more prosperous, and over time, an aristocracy, or group of wealthy people rose. These were mostly the people who controlled trade in the rich, rice-growing regions of Southeast Asia.

The aristocracy had much more contact with people from other parts of the world and began to adopt many of the beliefs, customs, and practices of other, more class-oriented societies. One of the customs that was adopted by the aristocracy was polygamy, or the practice of having more than one wife. The more wives you had, the wealthier you appeared to be. Some wealthy men collected wives in the same way wealthy people today might collect cars. These women were often treated like objects, and their main purpose was to produce children for their husbands. Sons were valued because sons would one day be loyal business partners who could expand the family fortunes. The only value a daughter might be was as a wife for a valuable business associate with whom one wanted to make permanent ties. Practices like polygamy marked a significant shift in women's status in Southeast Asian society.

In aristocratic societies, women no longer occupied positions of power within the family. The only woman who might have a position of power would be the first wife. Sometimes a first wife might continue to be a financial manager and play an important business role, but sometimes her power might simply be limited to having superiority over the other wives. Secondary wives and concubines had no rights whatsoever. They did not even have a right to their

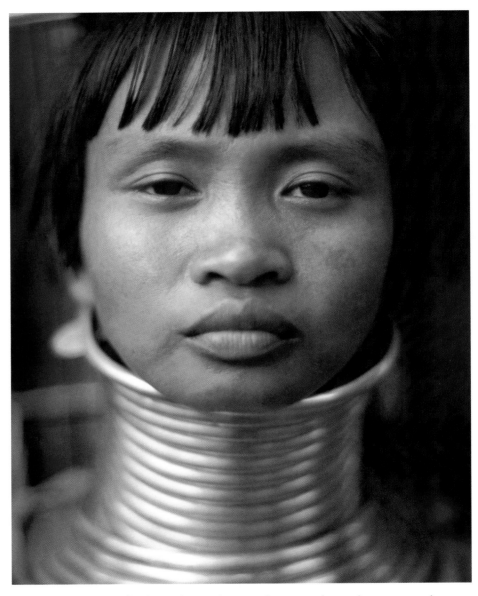

Women from some Southeast Asian tribes wear heavy metal rings that compress their shoulders, making their necks appear elongated.

own children. All the children would be considered those of the first wife, regardless of who their biological mother was.

In the late nineteenth and early twentieth centuries, when colonial powers brought huge numbers of workers from other areas into Southeast Asia, social structures shifted even more. Many of these workers came from places where polygamy was practiced by more than just the wealthy classes. The practice of polygamy and the inequality it brought to women's lives spread even further throughout Southeast Asian society.

To make matters worse, as the colonial powers took family farms and turned them into large plantations, many women lost their land—land that had previously allowed them independence and security. As most Southeast Asians grew poorer under colonial rule, and other options for making a livelihood decreased, many women turned in desperation to prostitution to support themselves and their families. This problem would only get worse in the future when much of Southeast Asia was ravaged by war. During wars, farmland was destroyed, men had to leave their communities to fight, and many women were left with no land to farm, no husband to help work, and children to feed or parents to take care of. Prostitution became the only option for many women, and soldiers with military paychecks provided a steady stream of income for prostitutes.

Another struggle for women in Southeast Asia has been education. In colonial Southeast Asia, often the only way to advance in society was through a European-style education, but this type of education cost money. Likewise, in European society it was men, not women, who held positions in business, scholarship, law-making, and government. Therefore, if a Southeast Asian family could only afford to educate one child, it made much more sense to educate a son rather than a daughter. Sometimes girls attended elementary school, but girls in lower-class families often received no education at all. Many other Southeast Asian girls left school at a young age and worked to make money for their brothers' education. This pattern of young women working to support men's education continues in many places today. Furthermore, in some areas of Southeast Asia, such as the Muslim population of Indonesia, there was another barrier that kept women from receiving an education. This was the practice of secluding girls when they reached puberty. Where seclusion was practiced, girls could interact in society freely until the age of about twelve. Once hitting puberty, however, girls were suddenly taken out of outside society and secluded in their homes to maintain their "purity" until marriage.

In the upper classes of Southeast Asian society, women did often receive an education, but this education also rarely went beyond age twelve. Furthermore, the purpose of this education was not the advancement of women. Rather, education for elite women was valued because it would make the woman a better wife and mother. A woman with a European-style education would be better equipped to help her husband advance in his career and would raise her children to function well in the upper echelons of society.

Not everyone in Southeast Asian society, however, thought that a woman's education was best used to serve her husband. One of Southeast Asia's first feminists was Raden Ajeng Kartini. Born in 1879, Raden Ajeng Kartini was the daughter of a Javanese official. As a member of the upper classes in Indonesia, Kartini received an education in a Dutch school. She had to stop going to school, however, when she reached puberty and was secluded. From her seclusion, Kartini wrote letters to her friends in Europe (friends she had met in school) describing the plight of women in Indonesia.

In her letters, Kartini wrote of the unfairness of secluding girls and denying them an education. She denounced marriage and polygamy. She valued education highly and thought a woman should be able to use her education in more productive ways than simply advancing her husband's career. In Kartini's time, however, the only option available to a young woman in Indonesia was marriage and motherhood. Kartini herself had very little interest in either, but she also

These Vietnamese girls will face prejudice as they grow older, simply because they are females.

Indonesian women are accustomed to carrying baskets and other objects on their heads.

had no choice in the matter. She was forced into an arranged, polygamous marriage, and in her letters she spoke about the negative impact arranged marriages, polygamy, lack of education, and inequality had on women's lives. In her quest to see change brought about in her society, Kartini began a school in her home. In 1904, however, at the age of just twenty-five, Kartini died in childbirth.

Kartini's letters and opinions may not seem so radical to us today, but in a time when many women could not even read or write and had no power over things like marriage, Kartini's opinions and desires for change were quite radical. Though she died very young, Kartini's memory lives on in Indonesia and around the world. Each year, Indonesia celebrates a holiday in Kartini's honor, and women's organizations hold her up as an example for women.

Women's strength in Southeast Asian society has also led them to occupy some unexpected roles. In some parts of Southeast Asia, women even became military leaders. One example of a military heroine is Tjoet Nyak Dhien. In their article, "Tjoet Nyak Dien: Queen of Jihad," Br. Benny Ohorella and Sr. Zaynab El-Fatah summarize Dhien's life.

Tjoet Nyak Dhien was born in 1848 to an Acehnese noble family. Her father and mother both came from military families, and her father was a commander for the Sultan's army. Though born into nobility, the Acehnese military would dominate Dhien's life, and eventually she would sacrifice all of her worldly possessions and comforts to its service.

At the time of Dhien's birth, the Dutch were the major colonial force in island Southeast Asia. Many people living in the islands that today make up Indonesia, however, refused to accept Dutch rule. In different Southeast Asian states, local armies were raised to fight the Dutch. As the years of war dragged on, these armies were pushed further and further into the jungles where they

A family in Myanmar outside of their home.

maintained constant guerilla operations hoping to one day overthrow their oppressive rulers. One of these guerilla units was led by Tjoet Nyak Dhien.

At the age of fourteen, Dhien married. Her husband was also an army commander. For the next ten years, her father and husband would fight the Dutch who sought to extend their colonial power over the state of Aceh. Eventually, however, the Dutch captured the Acehnese capital and the Acehnese army was forced into the jungle. In the following guerilla war, both Dhien's father and husband were killed. Upon their deaths, Dhien rounded the remaining troops from her father's and husband's armies. In the jungle, she rebuilt these Acehnese forces and continued the campaign against the Dutch.

Dhien later married another Acehnese army commander, and together they carried out a brilliant tactical move. They left their armies in the jungle (many of whom thought Dhien and her husband had become traitors) and surrendered to the Dutch forces. They acted repentant and told the Dutch they wished to help destroy the Acehnese. The Dutch were overjoyed and made Dhien's husband the commander of a Dutch army unit.

In their new role, Dhien and her husband were able to gather valuable information about the Dutch army and infiltrate the Dutch forces with their own Acehnese fighters. Dhien and her husband then deserted the Dutch army taking their Acehnese fighters, newly acquired knowledge, Dutch weapons, and military equipment with them. Back under the command of Dhien and her husband, the Acehnese guerilla armies were now greatly reinforced.

Dhien and her husband could not hold off the Dutch forces forever, and Dhien's husband was killed in 1899. Upon his death, Dhien returned to commanding her army, which was made up of both men and women, alone. By this time, Dhien was elderly, blind, and in declining health. She and her forces continued to fight from their location in the jungle until they were defeated in 1901. It is said that the Acehnese forces fought to the death for Dhien, and even when she was captured, Dhien held a dagger and struck out sightlessly

against her captors. The only member of Dhien's army not to be killed or captured was Dhien's daughter, Tjoet Gambang.

Tjoet Gambang disappeared further into the jungle. Very little is known about her life after her mother's capture, but like her mother, she continued to lead a guerilla army. It is believed that she died in the resistance in 1910.

Tjoet Nyak Dhien was taken to West Java where the locals never suspected that this small, religious woman had been one of the greatest resistance and military leaders against the Dutch. Though a prisoner of the Dutch army, Dhien became an instructor of Islam and came to be known by the locals as "Ibu Perbu" or "Great Queen." Tjoet Nyak Dhien died as a political prisoner in 1908.

The Samsui women were Cantonese women who left China in the early twentieth century to work abroad as laborers. The most famous and revered of these women was a group of about two thousand who settled in Singapore between 1934 and 1949.

The Samsui women came to Singapore searching for jobs and independence. Some fled arranged marriages in China. Others were simply looking for good-paying jobs. What set Samsui women apart from other immigrant women however, was their chosen trade. The Samsui women had been born into rural villages where they were expected to work alongside men in the fields. When they went abroad, instead of choosing the more traditional (and lower paying) jobs for women, they chose to become skilled manual laborers in construction.

The Samsui women, carrying loads of cement on their backs and working alongside men in the grueling and dangerous construction sites, became iconic figures in Singapore. They symbolized determination, hard work, strength, and independence. In a time when all women married, the Samsui women remained single.

A woman sells garlic from her boat in Southeast Asia.

Samsui women.

WOMEN IN THE WORLD OF SOUTHEAST ASIA

Despite their great physical strength and independence, the lives of Samsui women were extremely hard. They lived together in crowded conditions, sent all their money home to their families, faced great insecurity in their jobs, and eventually grew too old to perform heavy labor. Without husbands or family in Singapore, many returned to China where they were treated as strangers by their families. A few elderly Samsui women remain in Singapore today, eking out a living on their own selling vegetables or other goods. Some people are now trying to collect the histories of the Samsui women so their amazing lives and determination will never be forgotten.

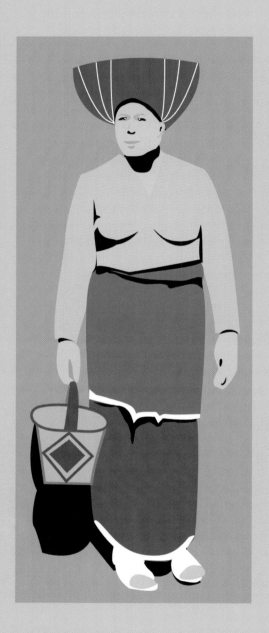

"THE MODERN WOMAN IN SOUTHEAST ASIA IS SMART, BOLD, CAPABLE, INDEPENDENT, AND NOT SUBORDINATE TO MEN."
—ONE MALAYSIAN WOMAN'S VIEW OF SOUTHEAST ASIAN WOMEN TODAY

WOMEN IN SOUTHEAST ASIA TODAY

Talking about women's lives in Southeast Asia today can be difficult because Southeast Asia does not have just one culture. Because of the many transformations the region has undergone throughout history, its current population is made up of numerous peoples with different languages, traditions, governments, beliefs, and histories. Even a single country can have many different ethnic groups and religions within its borders.

Just as the people of Southeast Asia have differences, however, they also have things in common, and there are many regional characteristics we can discuss. Think of this the way you would think of places like France and Germany. France and Germany are two very different countries. Their people speak different languages, eat different foods, and have different cultures. At times, France and Germany have even fought against each other in wars. Despite all these differences, however, France and Germany are part of a larger region— Europe. People of both countries participate in "European" culture. You can think of the United States and Canada in a similar way. There are many differences between these countries and their people. Yet both are part of North

America and its culture. Like Europeans and North Americans, the people of Southeast Asia have shared and continue to share many beliefs, experiences, and ways of life.

In most of Southeast Asia, the birth of a son is still greatly desired over the birth of a daughter. However, this has not stopped women in Southeast Asia from achieving great things. In Southeast Asia today, women play important roles in every level of society and the economy. Women are shopkeepers, educators, mothers, lawyers, doctors, and presidents, just to name a few.

In most places in Southeast Asia, both girls and boys are raised with the expectation that they will become productive, contributing members of the family. There are many ways to contribute productively to a family, but often this productivity comes in the form of earning money.

When it comes to earning money, women in Southeast Asia are very enterprising. They continue to manage the household's finances, run family businesses, and be entrepreneurs. Many women work more than one job. In some areas, it is becoming more common for women not to get married and instead to choose a single life and career path. It is also not unusual for a woman to earn more than their husband, though few people would openly advertise this fact.

In many areas of Southeast Asia, more women work outside of the home than work exclusively within the home. In rural areas, this work continues to be largely in the agricultural arena. In urban areas, women's jobs tend to be more diverse. One of the most common forms of employment for women in Southeast Asia is as shopkeepers or the heads of small family businesses. Women's dominance of trade continues to be a striking characteristic of women in Southeast Asia.

Economically speaking, women's lives in Southeast Asia today tend to be easier than they were one and two generations ago. Throughout the war years, women's lives were a terrible struggle as they tried to raise and feed families

A woman from Myanmar (Burma).

This woman is a flower seller in Rangoon, Myanmar.

alone. Jobs were scarce, lives were disrupted, invading armies seized the people's land, and men were gone to fight. Furthermore, in countries like Vietnam, Laos, and Cambodia many women and children were killed. Countries emerging from war faced numerous economic and political problems, and women and men struggled to put their lives back together. Today, Southeast Asian countries tend to be much more stable. There are more jobs for both women and men, and a woman can typically earn more at one job today than her grandmother could have earned working three jobs fifty years ago.

However, in both rural and urban areas, women continue to face barriers to their advancement in the economic sector. The top positions in business, law, health care, administration, and government are still dominated by men. Women also face wage discrimination by being paid less than men for performing the same job. Sometimes women only make half the wages men make for equal work.

How much a woman is able to achieve in Southeast Asia is still largely determined by the place in society in which she is born. If she is born in an area with good schools and a strong economy, she will have better prospects for her future. If she is born into a family that does not value the education of women, it will be more difficult for her to achieve. If she is born into a successful business or political family, she will likely be able to go as far as her desires and abilities can take her.

From an official point of view, Southeast Asian countries have extremely egalitarian societies. For example, Indonesia's 1945 constitution states, "women and men have the same rights and obligations within the family, society, and development." Many other Southeast Asian countries have similar statements of equality in their own constitutions.

Furthermore, countries throughout the region have passed many progressive laws to protect women both in the family and in society.

Laws that forbid polygamy, guarantee equal wages to men and women, make it illegal for women to be fired from a job due to pregnancy or marital status, make education compulsory for all children, and protect women from domestic violence are common in Southeast Asia. Having constitutional statements of equality and laws to protect women's rights, however, does not necessarily ensure that these ideals will become manifest within society. There are many ways in which everyday life in Southeast Asia differs from what is required by law.

Like a woman's access to education and employment, a woman's legal status and rights in Southeast Asia often depend on where she is born and what culture she is part of. In Singapore, for example, polygamy is illegal except for the Muslim community. The Muslim community, however, maintains its own laws for marriage and divorce, and according to Muslim law, a man can have up to four wives at one time.

Another example of the difference between official law and reality is the fact that despite being illegal in many areas, wage discrimination is still common. Discrimination in hiring is also common. Sometimes employers assume that a young woman will get married, have children, and quit her job or become less productive. An employer with these ideas might choose to hire a man instead of a woman, even if the woman has equal or better qualifications for the job.

Sometimes gender discrimination is also tied to race and ethnicity. For example, one Malaysian woman describes attitudes towards women in her country being influenced by ethnicity. She says that Malay and Indian women are often seen as more family oriented in keeping with their culture while Chinese women are seen as very driven and career-oriented due to their own culture. Employers who believe in such stereotypes will often prefer to hire a Chinese woman over a Malay or Indian woman. Such discrimination in wages and hiring may not be in keeping with legislation, but they are also very difficult to prove and fight against, especially when such beliefs and practices are prevalent in a given area.

Few men in these girls' tribe would marry a woman without the metal coils that create their concept of traditional beauty. As she grows older, the younger girl on the left will have more coils added to her neck by the older women of her tribe.

In Southeast Asia today, school is mandatory for both girls and boys through at least junior high. In some countries, both girls and boys complete much more education than this, while in other countries many children cease going to school after junior high.

Children like these in rural communities of Southeast Asia seldom have the opportunity to attend schools. Those who do have access to a school may not be able to afford to attend, since most schools require families to pay for school uniforms and school supplies.

It is often rural communities in which children receive fewer years of education. Many rural communities do not have a school that goes beyond the junior high. Children who wish to have further education must go to boarding schools in other towns. This costs money, and the privilege may be reserved for the males in the family.

According to the United Nations, illiteracy rates in every Southeast Asian country continue to be much higher for women than for men, but many of these statistics reflect differences in the older generation rather than today's youth.

For the most part, boys and girls in Southeast Asia now receive equal amounts of elementary and secondary education. Fewer women receive university education than men, but this is also quickly changing. Families that can afford to do so often send their children to universities overseas in countries like England, Canada, and the United States. Social values acquired overseas re-

In almost all of Southeast Asia, uniforms are required when attending school. Uniforms tend to be strict, with boys wearing pants, a button-down shirt, and short hair and girls wearing a skirt of appropriate length, a button-down shirt, and their hair tied back with an appropriately colored hair-tie. School uniforms reinforce what is socially accepted as appropriate dress for girls and boys.

garding women's independence have had an impact on women's lives in Southeast Asia, and feminist movements in Southeast Asia have been greatly tied to feminist movements in western countries.

Both women and men in Southeast Asia tend to be more reserved, especially with each other, than they are in North America or other western countries. Women and men do not hug or kiss in public. For some communities, it is inappropriate for women and men to even touch in public. Dating used to be a group event (if it happened at all). Groups of young men and women would socialize together, but not alone. In some countries, western-style dating is becoming common with today's young people.

Although there is a definite trend towards putting off marriage until one is older, many women in Southeast Asia continue to marry at a relatively early age. It was once common to see brides who were sixteen years old or even younger. Now such young brides are quite rare, but it is still common for women to marry while in their late teens.

Arranged marriages also continue to be common, especially among Indian and Malay populations. Many people in Southeast Asia tend to take a pragmatic approach to marriage rather than the romantic ideal valued in places like North America. Love is often expected to come later in a marriage rather than right at the beginning. Young people today, however, are demanding a say in their marriage partners more and more, but the family's approval is still highly valued. In some areas, marriage between ethnic groups is growing, especially in areas where people feel strong ties to their national identity rather than to just their ethnic identity.

Many things can change for a woman when she gets married. She now has a different relationship with her family and community. She takes on new responsibilities in the household. Her husband may have certain expectations for what she will do and how she will behave. Marriage can bring a new level of

A Malaysian woman wears the traditional attire of her region.

status for women, but in some cases it can also mean the end of education, a previous social life, or work outside of the home.

In some ways, one could say that women have progressed in Southeast Asian society, but some men have not. Women value their roles outside the home, but men often value traditional roles for women and want a traditional wife. Sometimes men feel threatened by the advances women have made. In Singapore, for example, there is even a trend for men to go to China in search of more docile, submissive wives than they can find at home. Balancing their desires for education and meaningful employment with social expectations and desires for marriage and family is clearly on of the biggest challenges facing Southeast Asian women today.

In Singapore, gender relations are complicated by conscription, which requires every Singaporean complete two years of mandatory military service. This time in the military puts young men behind women in education and the workforce. Upon completing military service, some men find themselves at a disadvantage compared to their female peers who have spent the two years furthering their education or gaining work experience.

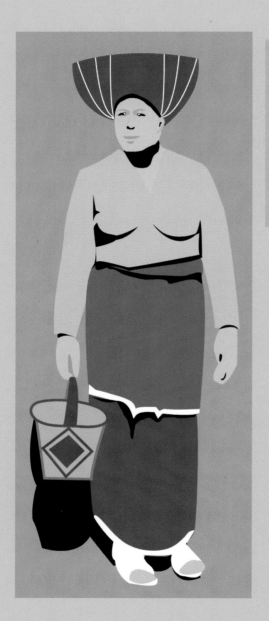

"MODERN INVENTION HAS BANISHED THE SPINNING WHEEL, AND THE SAME LAW OF PROGRESS MAKES THE WOMAN OF TODAY A VERY DIFFERENT WOMAN FROM HER GRANDMOTHER."
—SUSAN B. ANTHONY

4

WOMEN'S DUAL ROLE

Women in Southeast Asia today are asking the same question being asked by women all over the world. "How can we have it all?" Having a family is a full-time job, but many women want careers as well. Even if a woman would rather stay home and raise children, many Southeast Asian women are forced by economic circumstances to find employment and additional sources of income. The majority of women in Southeast Asia today have dual roles—a "traditional" role within the family and a "modern" role in the workforce.

There is a certain amount of tension surrounding women's dual roles in Southeast Asia today. In many areas, a traditional role for women is still highly valued. According to many people, the ideal woman is a good wife, mother, and keeper of the house. She is able to support her husband, giving him stability, love, and peace of mind so he can pursue his duties with strength and clear-headedness. She raises good and healthy children who will be able to support the family as adults, and she manages the household and finances in a way that always ensures the highest physical and mental health possible for the family. In this role, the ideal woman lives a life of service in which she is most

Women in Southeast Asia are usually responsible for preparing food for their families.

concerned with the health and happiness of others rather than of herself, and it is thought that leading this type of life will cause a woman natural happiness.

The above picture of the ideal woman is one that many people value around the world. If you asked most women, however, they would tell you that real-life is very different from this rosy picture and few women today can live up to the ideal, let alone be made happy by it. Furthermore, this ideal picture omits the important roles women have always played outside of the home. Though women's role in the family has always been important in Southeast Asian society, women were not traditionally confined exclusively to the home. Southeast Asian women have worked outside of the home for centuries. Attempts to confine women to home- and family-oriented roles are often not as much an attempt to preserve women's "traditional" roles as they are a reaction from conservative elements of society against social changes that have occurred in recent years. People who feel that society is changing too rapidly, who believe that too many Western values are being adopted, and who feel nostalgic for the way things were in the past may promote a "traditional role" for women that is in reality more restrictive than the roles women have historically had.

When people think of a woman's role in the family, they often think of a woman cooking, cleaning, and balancing a baby on her hip. Women's importance within families, however, goes far beyond these responsibilities.

One of the most important functions that women have always played within their families and society is cultural transmission, or the passing on of beliefs, values, family history, and cultural practices from one generation to the next. The women who stay home caring for children are not simply babysitting, they are also teaching these children about their history and culture.

In many ways, cultural transmission is more important in Southeast Asia now than it has ever been before. Many people's lives have been disrupted by years of war. Communities in Cambodia, Laos, Myanmar, Timor-Leste, and other places in Southeast Asia have faced genocide. People fleeing persecution and genocide continue to live in refugee camps in Thailand and other countries.

Today, there is a generation of young people who have been born in refugee camps and have never known the lands and original ways of life of their people.

Another threat to the survival of certain cultures in Southeast Asia comes from deforestation and destruction of the environment. For aboriginal peoples who have continued to live in the mountains, forests, and islands of Southeast Asia, destruction of the land by logging companies, plantations, mines, oil fields, and other commercial interests has meant the loss of customs and ways of life that have carried on for tens of thousands of years. In situations like these, the role of cultural transmission that women have traditionally played is more important than ever to the continued survival of the community. This is not to say, however, that men do not also play an important and increasingly indispensable role in cultural transmission. Men also have an important role to play, but it is women who manage the household and spend the most time with the children. It is therefore women who often have the greatest influence on the next generation.

With the need to work outside of the home, women have less time to spend with their children. The close-knit family structure of Southeast Asian society helps many women as they try to balance their dual roles of work and family. Even if most of the married women within a family are working outside of the home, there will often be an aunt or a grandmother who stays home to watch the children. However, as Southeast Asian populations move to urban areas and

Many women in Southeast Asia make additional money for their families by doing handiwork that can be sold in local or foreign markets.

A Thai woman and her children wear the colorful embroidered clothing traditional for her people.

The Hmong are just one group of people who were forced from their native land in China, settled in various portions of Southeast Asia, and continue to have their lives disrupted by persecution and war. Many Hmong people still reside in refugee camps, and in these camps they have started a new mode of cultural transmission known as the story cloth. Hmong women have long been known for their beautiful embroidery, and on these story cloths, Hmong women embroider pictures that record the histories of their communities. These story cloths will be passed on to future generations so the histories will not be forgotten. Although embroidery is traditionally done by women, many Hmong men in the refugee camps are also now contributing to the story cloths.

as household wealth increases, many people are living farther away from their families and in single-family houses. In this new situation, it is very common for working women of the middle and upper classes to have live-in maids or other employees who help raise the children and manage the house. Help like this, however, is a luxury that many women cannot afford.

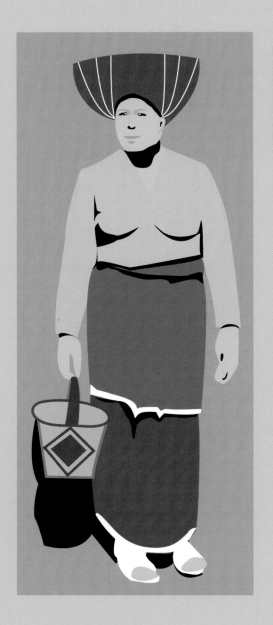

"THERE IS NO OCCASION
FOR WOMEN TO CONSIDER
THEMSELVES SUBORDINATE
OR INFERIOR TO MEN. "
—MOHANDAS K. GANDHI

RELIGION'S ROLE IN THE LIVES OF SOUTHEAST ASIAN WOMEN

Religion has a major influence on women's lives in Southeast Asia. This region is home to many different religions, and the effects they have on women's lives vary from religion to religion and community to community. The most common religions in Southeast Asia are Islam, Buddhism, Hinduism, and Christianity, though other religions are also practiced.

Islam is a religion based on the teachings of the Prophet Muhammad who lived in the seventh century. People who practice Islam are called Muslims. They believe in one god whose name is Allah. Their holy scriptures are the Qur'an (also spelled Koran), but portions of the Judeo-Christian Bible are also important to Islamic tradition.

In Southeast Asia today, more people practice Islam than any other religion. In fact, the country of Indonesia has the largest Muslim population in the world. Brunei-Darussalam and Malaysia also have majority-Muslim populations. Despite the fact that more Muslims live in Southeast Asia than in any other part of the world, the images of Islam that we are most familiar with in

71

A Thai woman wears a traditional headdress, connecting her to her family's past.

WOMEN IN THE WORLD OF SOUTHEAST ASIA

North America are of Islam as it is practiced in the Middle East. Islam has historically taken a different form in Southeast Asia.

One of the ways in which Islam is different in Southeast Asia than in the Middle East is in its attitude towards women. Islam in the Middle East has come under great criticism for the frequent maltreatment of women in Islamic societies and the use of Islamic scripture as an excuse for such maltreatment. In many places in the Middle East, women have long been forced into subordinate and powerless positions. In some places, women are confined to their homes, forbidden to speak to men who are not members of their families, denied an education, required to cover their faces in public, and severely punished, even killed, for the most minor transgressions. In Southeast Asia, attitudes towards women in Islamic societies did not take these strict forms. Even though Islamic teachings officially disapprove of female leaders, women like the queens of Aceh and Tjoet Nyak Dhien were able to rise to positions of influence, power, and even military leadership. Women occupied positions of authority in their families, and the restrictive veils so common in the Middle East and publicized in the West were uncommon in Southeast Asia.

Today in Southeast Asia however, there is an increasing trend in conservative attitudes towards women in Muslim communities. Head scarves, though long-worn in many Muslim communities, are becoming the rule in some communities where they were not previously required. In addition, the veils covering women's faces, before unseen in Southeast Asia, are also becoming common in some areas.

Buddhism is the second largest religion in Southeast Asia. Buddhism is the major religion practiced in Thailand, Myanmar, Cambodia, Lao People's Democratic Republic, and Vietnam. This religion is based on the teachings of Buddha, or the Enlightened One. The Buddha began his life as Siddhartha

Gautama, an Indian prince who lived from 563 to 483 B.C.E. Siddhartha Gautama renounced all his worldly goods and set out on a path to find freedom from suffering. According to the Buddha's teachings, all living things are caught in a cycle of rebirth into the world of suffering. The only way to end suffering and rebirth is to remove all desire (the cause of suffering) and thus obtain enlightenment.

Buddhism affects women's lives in Southeast Asia in different ways. On the one hand, Buddhists believe in an egalitarian society. Buddhists stress the importance of doing good deeds and respecting all living things. In many Buddhist's eyes, men and women are equal. These beliefs benefit not only women but all people in a society. However, sometimes Buddhism affects women's lives in a different way.

Although some Buddhists see women and men as equals, others believe women are more connected to the world of suffering and are lesser beings than men. Buddhist monks and nuns are greatly respected in Southeast Asian society, but in some places, Buddhist nuns spend their lives cooking and cleaning for the monasteries of monks rather than spending their lives in religious contemplation as prescribed by their religion.

Another hardship for Buddhist women can be created by the fact that in Buddhist society it is acceptable for men to leave their families behind to become monks. A man may "go forth" to become a monk temporarily (he may study for weeks, months, or years before returning to his family) or he may go forth permanently. In Thailand, for example, the majority of men will go forth as a monk at some point in their lives. A man's going forth is always seen as a positive, joyful event, but many men leave wives and children behind. A woman whose husband has gone forth is not supposed to resent her husband's absence, but caring for a family alone is a great burden that many women face.

Hindu deities are often female.

Hinduism is also practiced throughout Southeast Asia, though it is not nearly as prevalent as it once was. Brought to Southeast Asia by the Indian community, Hinduism is a religion of numerous male and female gods. Like Buddhists, Hindus believe that we are all caught in a cycle of rebirth. One's actions in this life determine the type of life one will be born into next. Through correct action towards others and the gods, one can eventually be freed from the cycle of rebirth.

Unlike Buddhism, Hinduism is caste-oriented; meaning at the foundations of the religion is a belief in different castes, or classes, in society. A person born into a lower caste can never move into a higher caste. The only way to improve one's position within society is to live well and be reborn into a better life. In Hinduism, there is also a division between men and women, men being seen as higher beings and dominant over women.

The only Southeast Asian countries in which Christianity is a majority religion are the Philippines and Timor-Leste. Christian religions are based on the belief that the Jewish teacher, Jesus of Nazareth, was the son of God. According to Christianity, Jesus was sent to earth as a sacrifice to redeem the human race from its sins so that humans could once again reside with God in heaven. This religion was brought to Southeast Asia by Spanish missionaries.

Christianity is a religion that takes many different forms throughout the world. Different local practices and beliefs are often absorbed into Christianity, and Christian religions can vary greatly from place to place. Many of the ways in which Christianity affects a woman's life, therefore, has as much to do with the way Christianity is adopted to her particular culture's belief systems as to specific teachings within the Bible. According to the Christian Bible, women should obey their husbands, both men and women should be virtuous and without sin, and both men and women should abstain from sexual relations before marriage.

Southeast Asia is a land of ancient faith.

Before Islam, Buddhism, Hinduism, and Christianity arrived in Southeast Asia, the major form of religion was animism. Animism continues to be the basis for religious belief for many aboriginal peoples in Southeast Asia. Furthermore, many Christian, Hindu, Buddhist, and Muslim communities throughout the region still have traces of animism that have survived and been absorbed into these other religions.

Animistic societies believe that everything in the world, living and non-living alike, has a spirit. Both women and men in animistic societies live with a great respect for their surroundings and for the natural world. Animism is not an organized religion in the way that religions like Islam and Hinduism are. Therefore, animism can take many different forms among different groups of people.

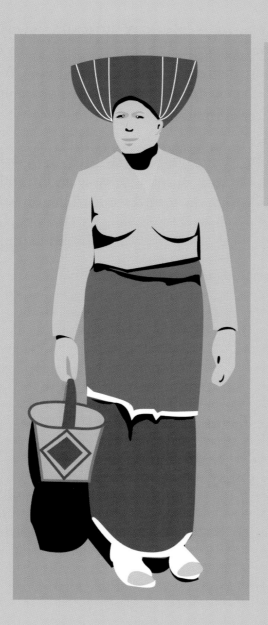

"JOIN ME AS WE BEGIN TO
TEAR DOWN THE WALLS
THAT DIVIDE. LET US
BUILD AN EDIFICE OF
PEACE, PROGRESS, AND
ECONOMIC STABILITY."
—GLORIA MACAPAGAL
ARROYO

WOMEN IN THE PUBLIC EYE

It was nighttime, and the group of people moved down the road towards the house where they would rest for the night. Suddenly, up ahead, they saw soldiers. The soldiers kneeled in the road and shouted that the people could not pass. One lone woman stepped from the crowd and continued walking calmly down the road. The soldiers trained their guns on the woman and warned that they would shoot, but she did not stop. They began counting down, but still Aung San Suu Kyi proceeded towards the guns.

In Southeast Asia, women have served and continue to serve their countries and their people in important and dramatic ways. At a time when a developed nation like the United States has yet to even seriously consider a female president, the nations of Southeast Asia have had numerous female leaders. These women have made history, not only in Southeast Asia, but also in the world.

Aung San Suu Kyi is the leader of the National League for Democracy (NLD), a political party that has been fighting for democracy in Myanmar since 1988. Her now-famous walk towards the soldiers' guns is representative

of the strength and courage with which she has led Myanmar's struggle against the military authorities. Suu Kyi has sacrificed much in the fight for human rights and democracy in Myanmar, and in 1991 she was awarded the Nobel Peace Prize for her efforts.

Aung San Suu Kyi was born in 1945, the daughter of the famous General Aung San who led Burma to independence from colonial rule. General Aung San was assassinated in 1947, and Burma was unable to achieve the democracy to which General Aung San and other leaders had aspired. Instead, a military dictatorship eventually took hold.

Aung San Suu Kyi was just two years old when her father was assassinated. Though she could not remember her father, she would one day strive to walk in his footsteps. Suu Kyi was educated first in India and then in England. She married an Englishman, Michael Aris, and had two children. Completely unaware that she was destined to become Myanmar's most important leader, Suu Kyi lived happily for a number of years caring for her family in England.

In 1988, however, Aung San Suu Kyi's life changed quickly and would never be the same. Upon receiving word that her mother was extremely ill, Suu Kyi returned to Burma. At this same time, a series of student protests had turned into bloody massacres at the hands of the Burmese army. Each day the protests grew, and each day the military's reaction grew more brutal. The number of dead rose quickly, and thousands of people were imprisoned. Soon it looked like Burma would descend into civil war.

Aung San Suu Kyi decided it was time to enter the fight. She called a rally of the people, and was astonished when more than 500,000 showed up to hear her speech. She told the people that they needed to unite behind two things—a call for democracy and a commitment to nonviolence. Thus, the National League for Democracy was born with Suu Kyi as its leader. It quickly rose to be the most popular political party in Myanmar, and many credit Suu Kyi with saving the country from civil war.

WOMEN IN THE WORLD OF SOUTHEAST ASIA

Children in Myanmar look down from a window. Aung San Suu Kyi worked hard to create a better nation for children like these.

Aung San Suu Kyi

In response to pressure from the international community, the military dictatorship of Myanmar promised to hold free, multi-party elections. Upon seeing how popular the NLD was becoming, however, the government realized it would lose these elections. Aung San Suu Kyi was placed under house arrest, other party leaders were imprisoned, and the NLD was removed from the ballots. Nevertheless, the military government and the world were stunned when on May 27, 1990 Aung San Suu Kyi's oppressed and imprisoned party won a landslide victory by receiving more than 80 percent of the vote. The military regime, faced with losing its power, tightened its hold on the country, declared the results of the election void, and continued its oppression of the people. Aung San Suu Kyi remained under house arrest, and the other NLD leaders remained in prison.

Aung San Suu Kyi's house arrest continued until 1995. Upon her release, she immediately returned to political activity, holding weekend meetings at her home where hundreds of people would come to hear her speak and traveling throughout the country working for the cause of democracy. Seeing that her popularity and influence remained strong, the military eventually forbade Suu Kyi's weekend speeches. Her house arrest was later imposed again, and today her movements continue to be restricted by the military government. All information going in and out of the country is also restricted.

Since 1988, Aung San Suu Kyi has rarely been able to see her sons. When her husband, Michael, was dying of cancer, the government of Myanmar refused to grant him a visa to see his wife one last time. Knowing that if she left the country she would never be permitted to return, Suu Kyi chose to stay in Myanmar. Michael died on March 27, 1999 without being able to see his wife one last time. Despite the suffering she has faced, Suu Kyi continues to work for the people of Myanmar. She believes that the suffering of the Burmese people is much greater than anything she has been forced to endure, and that this

Corazon Aquino.

suffering will not end until democracy and peace are brought to this oppressed land.

* * *

Born in 1933 in the Philippines, Corazon Aquino spent much of her adult life fulfilling the role of mother and wife. Few would have guessed that this woman would one day overthrow a powerful dictator, become president of the Philippines, survive numerous coup attempts, and help to restore order and hope to an ailing country.

Corazon Aquino, however, has done all of these things. At first, she had no desire for political leadership. She was content to support her husband, Benigno Aquino Jr., as he led a popular opposition party against the Philippine's dictator, Ferdinand Marcos. In 1972, Benigno was imprisoned. In 1977, he was given a death sentence, but in 1980, Benigno and Corazon were permitted instead to leave the country in exile. Benigno returned to the Philippines in 1983, only to be assassinated in the Manila airport.

Upon her husband's death, Corazon Aquino was thrust into the position of opposition leader. At first she was not enthusiastic about entering politics, but it soon became clear that no one else could unite and galvanize the opposition against Marcos. In 1986, backed by the People Power revolution, Corazon ran against Marcos for the presidency of the Philippines. At first, both Aquino and Marcos declared themselves winners of the election, but Marcos then fled the country.

Aquino fought many political battles in her six years as president of the Philippines. From the beginning, she was plagued by opposition from military leaders who themselves hoped to gain power and from people who believed a woman and former housewife could not possibly lead a country. To make matters worse, Aquino inherited a country struggling with political instability and a weak economy. A common criticism of Aquino is that she led a weak govern-

ment. Few people can deny, however, that in a time when democracy was close to failure in the Philippines, when communist guerillas and Muslim insurgents threatened civil war, and when the international community was loath to invest in the Philippine's economy, Aquino was able to hold the country together, restore democracy, begin a path to economic stability, and give the people hope for the future.

Unfortunately, many of the gains that President Aquino was able to make were undone by the presidents who followed her. Gloria Macapagal-Arroyo is the current president of the Philippines. She is the second woman to be brought into this position by the People Power revolution, and she too is trying to restore the order and stability that President Aquino strove for. The Philippines has continued to suffer political instability, a weak economy, rising crime rates, and rising poverty. When Arroyo became president in 2001, she hoped to curb the country's downward slide and restore faith in the government.

Born in 1947, Arroyo is the daughter of former Filipino president Diosdado Macapagal. Arroyo studied in the Philippines and the United States and holds a Ph.D. in economics. She served as Assistant Secretary of Trade and Industry under President Corazon Aquino. In 1992, she was elected to the senate. She was re-elected in 1995, and was elected vice president in 1998. In 2001, then President Joseph Estrada resigned after being impeached, and Gloria Macapagal-Arroyo assumed the presidency.

Arroyo's success in the presidency of the Philippines remains to be seen. Thus far, she has survived one coup attempt, but been unable to restore economic or political stability.

Born in 1947, Sukarnoputri Megawati is the daughter of Indonesia's "founding father" Sukarno. She is the leader of the PDI-P, Indonesia's leading pro-democracy party, and is currently the country's president.

WOMEN IN THE WORLD OF SOUTHEAST ASIA

Gloria Macpagal-Arroyo

Sukarnoputri Megawati

Megawati shares many characteristics with her fellow female leaders in Southeast Asia. Like Gloria Macpagal-Arroyo, Sukarnoputri Megawati assumed the presidency of her country in 2001, following the impeachment of the former president, in this case President Abdurrahman Wahid. Like Corazon Aquino, Megawati traveled a long road to politics, being a wife and mother before beginning a political career. Like Aung San Suu Kyi, Megawati fought for democracy against a powerful government regime.

Also like her fellow female leaders in Southeast Asia, Megawati faces great challenges in her presidency. Like the Philippines, Indonesia is also plagued by political and economic instability. Like Myanmar, Indonesia has a powerful military and police force without the backing of which, a president is unlikely to maintain power for long. Whether Megawati will be able to lead her country to lasting stability, prosperity, peace, and democracy remains to be seen, but she has given her country new hope that government corruption can be curbed by the democratic process.

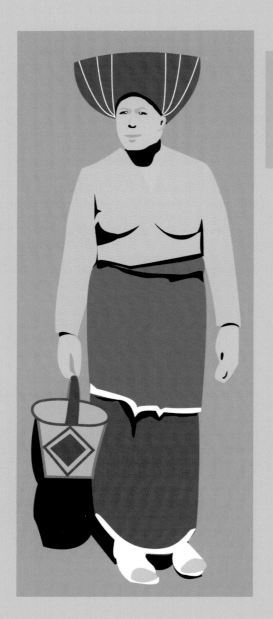

"WE WILL REACH OUR GOALS. IT MAY TAKE A LONG TIME, BUT WE WILL GET THERE."
—AUNG SAN SUU KYI

7

LOOKING TOWARD THE FUTURE

Despite the many things women have accomplished in Southeast Asia, they still face many struggles. The prevalence of prostitution and the dangers it causes in women's lives, the protection of female workers, and the elimination of poverty are some of the major challenges that will continue to be at the forefront of women's issues.

Prostitution continues to be a prevalent and dangerous occupation among women in Southeast Asia. In some countries, like Singapore, which has strict laws and a strong economy, prostitution is virtually nonexistent. In other countries, like Thailand and the Philippines, prostitution continues to be widespread.

Throughout Southeast Asia, millions of women and children are estimated to be working as prostitutes. Some women enter prostitution knowingly and willingly, but many women and children are tricked, sold, or even kidnapped into the sex trade. In Southeast Asia, it is common for women (especially women from the Philippines) to work in other countries as maids, nannies, and

Women in Southeast Asia often have few options for supporting their families.

other domestic workers. Many women are lured into the sex trade by dishonest business people. The women think they are going abroad as domestic workers, only to find when they arrive in the foreign country that they have actually been brought to work in prostitution. Prostitution in Southeast Asia has also become a foundation for some tourist industries.

Prostitution is closely connected to poverty. As long as Southeast Asian countries are unable to build strong economies and eliminate poverty, prostitution will remain the only viable option for many women. Furthermore, many countries have a difficult time curbing prostitution because it plays such a vital role in the country's overall economy. It is estimated that as much as 60 percent of Thailand's annual revenue may come from prostitution. Any activity that

Many countries in Southeast Asia have laws meant to protect domestic
workers abroad from improper treatment by their employers. You must, however, be eighteen years old to be a domestic worker abroad. Many young
women lie about their age, and when they are treated poorly by employers,
they cannot seek legal protection.

brings this much money into a country, no matter how harmful it may be to the
people involved, can be difficult for a country to eliminate.

Nevertheless, prostitution in Southeast Asia must receive greater attention
from governments, for the risks to people involved in the trade are too great.
Prostitution contributes greatly to the rapid spread of HIV, the virus that causes
AIDS, and other sexually transmitted diseases. Many Southeast Asian governments, burdened by wars, political upheaval, and economic instability, have not
paid a great deal of attention to the problem of HIV, and some people fear that
HIV in Southeast Asia may be spreading in epidemic proportions. Greater education about the causes and spread of HIV, greater access to the drugs that
treat HIV and AIDS, and greater regulation of the sex industry, combined with
a significant decrease in the number of people living in poverty will all help
Southeast Asia address this growing problem.

Female labor is important to the economies of many Southeast Asian nations.

There continues to be a gap between laws on the books meant to protect female workers from discrimination, injury, harassment, and abuse, and the carrying out of these laws in the workplace. These issues can be particularly difficult for governments to negotiate. Many aspects of Southeast Asian economies are driven by female labor. On the one hand, these women need equal protection under the law. On the other hand, greater regulation and a demand for

Women like these deserve equal protection under the law.

increased wages can cause employers to look for cheaper labor and operating costs elsewhere, leading to the loss of jobs and damage to the economy. This situation traps many women in a no-win situation in which the only choices are to be employed in a low-paying job with poor working conditions or to have no job at all.

As long as poverty drives people and governments to accept lower wages and poor working conditions out of desperation, the problem of unequal legal protection for women in the workforce will be difficult to solve. Southeast Asian countries are by no means the only countries facing this dilemma. Throughout the world, many countries find themselves in a catch-22—without safe, well-paying jobs, they cannot eliminate poverty. For as long as there is poverty, however, they are forced into settling for dangerous working conditions and low-paying jobs.

Around the world, scholars discuss a problem that has come to be known as the "female face of poverty." This phrase is often used to describe the fact that more women and children around the world live in poverty than men. This is thought to be caused by the fact that in many societies, men have more opportunities for work and education than women, are paid higher wages for the same jobs, have greater protection under the law, and are not responsible for the care of children in the same way that women are.

Poverty is rampant in many Southeast Asian countries, and in many of these areas poverty does indeed have a female face. As we have seen, poverty leads to many other dangers for women and society, and if the poverty situation improved, many other conditions would improve as well. Eliminating poverty is perhaps the greatest challenge facing Southeast Asia today, and it will continue to be a challenge long into the future.

Despite the many challenges women in Southeast Asia continue to face, there can be no doubt that Southeast Asian women are indeed strong, capable, inde-

pendent, and ready for the future. Southeast Asia has clearly had and continues to have a tradition of strong female leadership. As Southeast Asian countries move forward with the hope of more stability and prosperity in the future, women will continue to play an indispensable role in every aspect of society, from the family, to business, to government. Although women are still under-represented in the upper echelons of business and administration, some have successfully broken through the glass ceiling. These women continue to achieve for their families, communities, and countries, and pave the way for the women who will follow in the future.

FURTHER READING

Aung San Suu Kyi. *The Voice of Hope*. New York: Seven Stories Press, 1997.

Brown, Sid. *The Journey of One Buddhist Nun: Even Against the Wind*. Albany, New York: State University of New York Press, 2001.

Green, Robert. *Cambodia*. Farmington Hills, Miss.: Lucent Books, 2003.

Khng, Pauline. *Myanmar*. Milwaukee, Wisc.: Gareth Stevens Publishing, 2000.

Layton, Lesley and Pang Guek Cheng. *Singapore*. Tarrytown, New York: Marshall Cavendish Corporation, 2002.

Major, John S. *The Land and People of Malaysia & Brunei*. New York: HarperCollins Publishers, 1991.

Munan, Heidi and Foo Yuk Yee. *Malaysia*. Tarrytown, New York: Marshall Cavendish Corporation, 2002.

Nickles, Greg. Philippines, *The People*. New York: Crabtree Publishing Company, 2002.

Parenteau, John. *Prisoner for Peace: Aung San Suu Kyi and Burma's Struggle for Democracy*. Greensboro, North Carolina: Morgan Reynolds Inc., 1994.

Taylor, Jean Gelman. *Women Creating Indonesia: The First Fifty Years*. Victoria, Australia: Monash Asia Institute, 1997.

FOR MORE INFORMATION

The Asia Society: Ask Asia
www.askasia.org

Association for Asian Studies
www.aasianst.org

Daw Aung San Suu Kyi's Website
www.dassk.org

Gloria Macapagal Arroyo's Website
www.kgma.org

The Metropolitan Museum of Art: Timeline of Southeast Asian Art History
www.metmuseum.org/toah/splash.htm

Pan-Pacific and South-east Asia Women's Association International
www.ppseawa.org

Tjoet Njak Dien, "The Queen of Jihad" by Br. Benny Ohorella and Sr. Zaynab El-Fatah
www.1ummah.org/articles/queenofjihad.html

"Strong as Mountains, Free as Water: The Samsui Women" by Cheryl Sim, Singapore
www.geocities.com/Wellesley/3321/win9b.htm

The United Nations
www.un.org

United Nations Educational, Scientific and Cultural Organization
www.unesco.org

UNIFEM (United Nations Development Fund for Women)
www.unifem.org

Women of Southeast Asia
www.womenshistory.about.com/cs/southeastasia/

Publisher's note:
The Web sites listed on these pages were active at the time of publication. The publisher is not responsible for Web sites that have changed their addresses or discontinued operation since the date of publication. The publisher will review and update the Web sites upon each reprint.

GLOSSARY

aboriginal Being the first or earliest known of its kind present in a region.

accessible Providing access; capable of being reached.

archaeological Relating to the scientific study of material remains (as fossil relics, artifacts, and monuments) of past human life and activities.

atrocities Extremely wicked, brutal, or cruel acts, objects, or situations.

catch-22 A problematic situation for which the only solution is denied by a circumstance that is part of the problem.

class Social rank; especially, high social rank.

concubines Women with whom a man cohabits without being married; mistresses.

controversial Of, relating to, or arousing a discussion marked especially by the expression of opposing views.

coup A brilliant, sudden, and usually highly successful stroke or act.

denounced Pronounced, especially publicly, to be blameworthy or evil.

disillusioned Disenchanted; disappointed; dissatisfied.

diverse Different from one another; unlike.

double standard A set of principles that applies differently and usually more rigorously to one group of people or circumstances than to another.

echelon One of a series of levels or grades in an organization or field of activity.

egalitarian Asserting, promoting, or marked by a belief in human equality, especially with respect to social, political, and economic rights and privileges.

empires Major political units having territories of great extent or numbers of territories or peoples under a single sovereign authority.

entrenched Established solidly.

entrepreneurs Those who organize, manage, and assume the risks of a business or enterprise.

ethnic Of or relating to large groups of people classed according to common racial, national, tribal, religious, linguistic, or cultural origin or background.

feminists Those who promote the theory of the political, economic, and social equality of the sexes.

galvanize To stimulate or excite as if by electric shock.

genocide The deliberate and systematic destruction of a racial, political, or cultural group.

glass ceiling An intangible barrier within the hierarchy of a company that prevents women or minorities from obtaining upper-level positions.

guerilla A person who engages in irregular warfare, especially as a member of an independent unit carrying out harassment and sabotage.

iconic As an idol or object of uncritical devotion.

infiltrate To enter or become established in gradually or by going unnoticed, usually for subversive purposes.

insatiable Incapable of being satisfied; quenchless.

insurgents People who revolt against civil authority or an established government.

manifest Easily understood or recognized by the mind; obvious.

nostalgic Relating to a wistful or excessively sentimental yearning for return to or of some past period or irrecoverable condition.

oppression Unjust or cruel exercise of authority or power.

paddies Wet lands in which rice is grown.

pragmatic Relating to matters of fact or practical affairs often to the exclusion of intellectual or artistic matters.

prostitution The act or practice of indulging in promiscuous sexual relations, especially for money.

regional Affecting a particular administrative area, division, or district; localized.

rural Of or relating to the country, country people or life, or agriculture.

secluding Excluding from a privilege, rank, or dignity.

self-governance Government under the control and direction of the inhabitants of a political unit rather than by an outside authority.

staple Something having widespread and constant use or appeal.

stereotype Something conforming to a fixed or general pattern, especially a standardized mental picture that is held in common by members of a group

and that represents an oversimplified opinion, prejudiced attitude, or uncritical judgment.

successive Following in order; following each other without interruption.

terraces Series of horizontal ridges made in a hillside to increase cultivatable land, conserve moisture, or minimize erosion.

transgressions Acts, processes, or instances of infringing or violating a law, command, or duty.

urban Of, relating to, characteristic of, or constituting a city.

Western Of or relating to the culture of Europe and America.

INDEX

PICTURE CREDITS

BIOGRAPHIES

Autumn Libal is a freelance author and illustrator living in Vancouver, British Columbia. She received her degree from Smith College, an all women's college in Northampton, Massachusetts, where she developed a deep interest in women's issues. Autumn's writing has also appeared in *New Moon: The Magazine for Girls and Their Dreams,* as well as other Mason Crest series including, NORTH AMERICAN FOLKLORE and NORTH AMERICAN INDIANS TODAY.

Dr. Mary Jo Dudley is the director of Cornell University's Gender and Global Change Department, which focuses on the evolving role of gender around the world. She is also the associate director of Latin American Studies at Cornell.